Divine Redemption

A Poem By:

Jenny Chapman

Copyright © 2025 by Jenny Chapman

All rights reserved. No part of this publication may be reproduced, distributed, or transmitted in any form or by any means, including photocopying, recording, or other electronic or mechanical methods without permission from the publisher.

ISBN# 979-8-218-78561-1 (Ebook)

ISBN# 979-8-218-79883-3 (Paperback)

Library of Congress Control #1-14930182361

Photography by:

Jackie Schutza and Jenny Chapman

All scriptures quoted are from the King James Version, public domain

Book cover design and some illustrations in this poem were generated using Canva's AI tools and were edited and arranged by the author.

1st Edition

Contents

Preface……………………………………………… v

Miss Melancholy……………………………………...1

The Inner Child……………………………………….4

The Final Stage……………………………………….7

Yeshua (Salvation)..11

Redemption…………………………………………..14

Agape (God's love)..18

El Roi (The God who sees me)……………………....20

Acknowledgments…………………………………....22

Resources…………………………………………….24

About The Author…………………………………....25

Dedication
In Loving Memory of

Erik Brandon Parker

Megan Elizabeth Olson

Your love still echoes in the heartbeat of every life you've both touched in this world. Heaven gained two precious angels.

You are both loved and missed dearly!

Preface

Suicide is one of the leading causes of death globally, especially in adolescents which is heartbreaking! Mental health affects us on a physical and spiritual level too. Spiritual warfare is real and I'm ready to fight to end the stigma and give others hope.

I was at my lowest moment in 2014 after enduring eleven years of chronic PTSD and compassion fatigue working as a veterinary technician. I spent most of my career working in ICU and ER where I witnessed countless euthanasias, trauma and suffering with my patients. I was also there to support the families who dealt with the loss and grief of their beloved pet. I have such a compassionate heart that over time it became a heavy burden to carry. No one educated me on the importance of self care and therapy to take care of my own mental health. I had suicide ideation and planned to jump off the Golden Gate Bridge to end my emotional pain and haunting memories but then God intervened.

Within the span of 2017-2019, I would then experience mental health related losses of two veterinary colleagues, my childhood friend Megan and one of my soulmates Erik. They are both memorialized on my dedication page. My heart shattered but it also got me to wake up realizing I was heading down a road to the same fate. Grief became my battle cry, to be a voice in a world where people still suffer in silence.

I have always been a woman of faith, so I began to do something I hadn't done in a long time. I prayed and then God began to heal my heart.

I lived in San Francisco from 2011-2016. It's such a beautiful city to photograph in. The art, culture and nature are mesmerizing! But there was one place in particular that had a certain allure to it. The Golden Gate Bridge is famous for many reasons and sadly has been one of the top suicide destinations in America. The city recently installed a suicide barrier around the span of the bridge in hopes to prevent people from choosing it as their final destination.

I remember taking a boat tour in 2012 where I captured the photos that are published in this poem. As we approached the Golden Gate Bridge, I was in awe! It is definitely something to marvel at. I remember the tour guide saying something very sobering, "Please pray no one jumps off the bridge today." I didn't realize even then, God was in my story. As I prayed, I felt the Holy Spirit's presence as I saw a light beam down through the clouds ascending over the bridge. The picture I captured is in this poem under the title Yeshua (Jesus Christ).

In 2020 The Holy Spirit began helping me write my testimony. God told me in order to help others understand mental health and give people who struggle hope, my pain needed a voice too.

Throughout my poem you will see the semicolon in place of a period. This is on purpose. The semicolon has become a symbol of hope and for suicide awareness. It represents the continuation of a life that could have ended but decided to continue.

The Holy Spirit reminded me that we each have a lantern glowing inside of us, full of his love. Imagine we are all lighthouses and that love glowing is lamp oil and a beacon of hope for the lost souls who are in need of love and healing. I believe that if we accept God into our heart, we will always be able to navigate our way home to who we truly are, which is all-encompassing love!

"And we have known and believed the love that God hath to us. God is love; and he that dwelleth in love dwelleth in God, and God in him."

1 John 4:16 (KJV)

Take a voyage with me on my hero's journey and testimony of how I reconciled and restored my relationship with Jesus Christ when I was at my lowest moment feeling hopeless, lost and broken. Sometimes all it takes is a little faith to ignite the lighthouse within us to remember who we are.

Our true identity is not defined by our mistakes, our self-limiting beliefs, how society views us or our relationships. Our true identity is defined by a loving God who created the Heavens and Earth and he created us for a special purpose too. Place your hand over your heart, do you feel that? You are still here for a reason. Jesus loves us so much and we are meant to share that love with others. I believe we meet our true selves when we are able to surrender the shadow parts of who we are that we deem unworthy or unlovable to God. This allows Christ to begin to heal us in our emotional fragility.

Our lantern then becomes a little bit brighter and that love begins to glow. Our lamplight begins to radiate, becoming a beacon of hope for more people to shine in their authentic selves as well, as they feel seen and safe in our light. One by one our lighthouses radiate throughout the world, healing one soul at a time as we become instruments of God's love. Uniting as one voice, shifting into peace, love and joy! Get ready to pick up your lantern and let us begin the journey.

Miss Melancholy

I finally had enough one day, of enduring my suffering and devastating pain; I looked back at my past with hopelessness and despair; It seemed like no matter how hard I tried to succeed at life, I felt defeated and no one cared;

In my heart I knew what I had to do, even though I had no sense, not even a clue; That my journey would lead me through my darkness and pain, to help me overcome my shadows and fight to live again;

I was tired of running from all of my sins, as I mourned a life that could have been; I was tormented by sinister shadows that wouldn't let me win; I called them inner demons and they all had a name; Telling me I wasn't worthy of love, I called them shame, guilt and pain;

I had it all planned out or so I had thought; I knew when I saw it, my inner demons began to plot; I was in awe, it was so hauntingly beautiful! As I gazed at the bridge floating in the sky;

It was then that I knew I wanted to fly!

This bridge was famous and a part of history, yet it was such a mystery! I knew it would be a place to end my shame; It was known as,

The Golden Gate in the City by the Bay;

I called it dark beauty, a place to fade away;

A space of solace to quiet the noise, the chaos in my head, that resounding voice; This inner demon was insidious and caused me dread, that someday I just might be, better off dead;

Compelling voices convincing me I wasn't lovable, not even by God; A sinking notion that my life was just a facade; Not seen, valued or even capable; These feelings left me hopeless with a broken heart, bondage that seemed unbreakable;

I never thought this would be the turning point for me, as I began my long walk home to eternity; Feeling lost in isolation, melancholy and self loathing;

I just wanted to escape!

I was now ready to seal my fate;

The Inner Child

I approached the pathway that would lead me across the bridge; I looked ahead at the sun glowing along the looming ledge, It cast a glimmering hue against the tall, alluring tower; This gave me comfort knowing this would be my final hour;

As I walked further I suddenly didn't feel so alone; Yet I looked back only to find my own shadow following me to my eternal home;

I saw a silhouette of a girl draw closer to me, she felt familiar like I knew her before; As I began to look over the ledge down into the waves she began to implore, "Don't go! You are seen! Can you hear me?!" Such a still small voice that began to plea; I looked down at this sweet little child, her light was so innocent and pure yet so meek and mild;

She asked me to stay and sit with her for a while, and said, "Remember me? When life was carefree and you were surrounded by love? If you have forgotten who you are, simply look above! Stay with me and I promise you I will help you to see!"

It was then that I realized that little girl was me;

I was so young when my innocence was lost, left with insufferable pain;
My inner child tried to reassure me she could help me find joy again!

But as I looked back at my life, all I felt was shame; She then pleaded with fretful tears in her eyes, "Please don't leave me! I will help you find the courage to live again!"

She pulled at my heartstrings as I was about to reach my journeys end;

The Final Stage

My inner demons were relentless so no matter how much she plead, I knew in the end this was my destiny; I gripped the railing of the bridge as I began to climb over, knowing soon I would get some closure;

I took one last deep breath as I prepared to take my final leap; I looked back at my inner child as she continued to weep, for a life that could have been, should have been and would have been for me; I decided this was easier, my soul was ready to be set free;

I then closed my eyes in my moment of woe; I spread my arms as I let go of the bridges railing, as I began my journey flailing down to the turbulent waves swirling below;

At first my heart was racing I never felt so alive! But then it began to burn as I knew I was about to die; Spiraling faster and faster looking down at the vortex below, my life flashing before me;

Counting four seconds of free fall before I go;

Morbid thoughts racing through my head, realizing soon I would be quite dead! Knowing it was all because of my own demise; My soul began to shout out my battle cry, "God! Oh God, how did I get into this mess?!"

Thinking, I was just tired of hurting, as I felt my heart aching wanting to beat out of my chest; It was then that I realized I wanted to live and not die;

I simply lost that part of me, that knew how to fly;

I then shouted, "God what can I do now?! If only I had reached out for help, if only I knew how?!" As I finished counting, my soul felt torn apart; I thought, at least soon I can be at rest and heal my broken heart;

But before the count was over I felt anything but peace; I felt fear run through my veins, as I realized the chilling grave below was waiting to bury my soul with no relief;

The four second count was over as I dove into my personal hell; My inner demons captured my heart and inside of it they would dwell; The impact didn't kill me as I fell into the dark abyss; All I could hear was my inner demon whispering,

"You won't be missed!"

What happened next was short of a miracle to say the least, I thought by now my soul would be at peace; But only darkness consumed me I felt anything but rest, my inner demons clawing at me and tearing at my chest;

I began to scream in agony as I began to cry, "God! Please God I don't want to die!" There was no hope, or so I had thought; It was then that still small voice shouted,

"Look up!"

But I was so distraught! My mind racing as I thought, how could God allow me to suffer like this?! To feel forsaken with a shattered heart and feel so dismissed?!

Then suddenly, I heard the Heavens rolling like thunder, as I felt a sovereign hand from above pulling me out of the abyss;

Yeshua (Salvation)

I knew this man, he was my hero you see! It was the Holy Spirit, my Lord and Savior Jesus Christ, he came down from Heaven to redeem me!

When I was a child he was my best friend, I loved him with all of my heart and soul! He helped plant seeds of faith as he watched my spirit grow. I was a songbird flying on the swing, he made my heart soar as he taught me to sing; He told me that if I was ever in fear that my voice would be the key; That when I began to praise him, it would unlock God's melody; A perfect love that would cast out all fear, If I ever felt the enemy come near;

My heart reflected on this memory fondly; So with all of my courage and strength, I looked up with praise as I began to sing, "Jesus Christ my Lord and Savior please hear my plea! I know my salvation is in your love please rescue me; Help me break my chains and set my soul free!"

Suddenly, my soul began to fly! My inner demons lost their grip and they were about to find out why; Flames consumed them as they began to flee, as I turned to my inner demons and shouted, "In the name of Jesus Christ, I stand in his mighty power and rebuke thee!"

They bowed in defeat as I then said,

"I have the Holy Spirit in my heart now, get behind me!"

The flames were extinguished as my Savior stepped in; It was then that I knew the enemy wasn't going to win; Like a bolt of lightning Christ beamed down shining bright! My heart finally knew I had found my light! I felt a soft warm glow, such love and peace;

All I felt around me was a sense of relief;

His glory shined upon me as I continued to sing his praise! I felt his wings of protection envelope me as I fell into his loving embrace; I then surrendered to the Prince of Peace as I knew I was safe in this Heavenly place!

The Holy Spirit said, "My sweet child return to me, for I am the way, the truth and the life! The doorway leading to eternity; It is now time to live and be free!"

Redemption

As a breath of life was given back to me, one thing I didn't expect to see, was that I was back at the bridge's railing;

A place fate meant for me to be;

As I opened my eyes as I looked around in disbelief; My life had flashed before me, didn't I just leap?! I felt a tug at my leg and looked down at my inner child as she said with a smile, "Will you stay and sit with me for awhile?"

We both embraced as tears of elation ran down her face; I wiped away her gentle tears and said, "I will never abandon you again!" I was comforted knowing I had found my new best friend;

She then looked up at me as she said with enthusiasm, "I was trying to tell you but you didn't believe! You have the courage of a lion as God helped you to see, Christ is the breaker of chains and his love set you free!"

The Holy Spirit's resounding voice stepped in to say, "My dear child now you see, In order to feel my love you need only to embrace me; I sent you here on earth to help you understand, now walk with me and take my hand;

"I am the Good Shepherd ready to lead and have wonderful plans for your life; Let me heal the pain that has caused you strife; Listen to my voice whisper in your heart to follow me, let me show you a life that is meant to be; A life full of love, joy and peace! Now that you have awakened, help others see; You were always meant to shine, not hide in the dark; So start to look within and find your spark; That part of me inside of you that no one can divide; My child, don't you see?

" You were never broken inside!"

"It's time to let go of the lies you believed were true; You were just ashamed and scared but I never abandoned you; It's time to step into your authenticity and be unique; For I set you apart and that is how I made you to be; You are a survivor and my warrior, now don't you see? You are born again as you were made in the likeness and image of me;

"Now carry your torch into other's darkness and their pain, help them ignite their beacon and live with purpose again; For you are all lighthouses meant to shine so bright! Guiding others home to harbor, safe in my light; Show them kindness, mercy and grace; Forgive them as I do, for I want to call all of my children home to my loving embrace!

"I will dispel all of your darkness as you step into my light; To help you live in blissful freedom, this is how you will fight; All of the evil in this world, as I heal your suffering and pain; Keep walking with me and I will help you live fully again!"

With joyful tears in my eyes, my inner child shined bright! I surrendered all of my darkness as it faded into God's light; My shadows I allowed to define me were no longer on display; With God walking by my side, surrounded by his glory, I'm much stronger today;

As I looked back contemplating what would have been my fate, my heart was raptured by a loving God who saved my life today; With my shadows cast behind me and my inner child and I walking hand in hand, I knew God had a purpose for my life and that he had a plan; Just like he does for all of his children, as there is never a soul too hidden from his love;

For we are all his precious treasures sent from Heaven above!

Agape (God's Love)

I then heard one last triumphant sound, as I continued to walk with Christ heading homeward bound; Like a lion's roar it was his battle cry! A message for his children and I began to see why;

A message so profound it brought me to tears, knowing I could have been saved from so many wasted years; You see, my purpose is to shine brighter than I ever did before!

Like a lighthouse, I'm now a beacon,

guiding lost souls safely home to shore;

This was the message that came through, as God's unfailing love began to speak truth; The Holy Spirit said, "Tell my children I will always meet them where they are; Even in their darkest moments, I will not forsake them, for I am never too far; So if they ever come face to face with their inner demons, tell them to repent and look within; For they are simply being guided to a part of their soul that needs healing; An emotional wound known as sin; But what does sin stand for anyway? Simply, 'Missing the mark;' In other words, misplaced faith and a longing for God's love in their hearts;"

The Holy Spirit continued to say, "Your inner demons wanted to separate you from me, they were after your heart, you see? They wanted to destroy everything good I made in you and kept you prisoner but my unconditional love set you free! You are perfectly imperfect as God gave you the choice of free will; That was what the enemy knew to be true and was trying to steal; But you withstood the trials and gained faith as you grew; Now start to live free as you are reborn brand new! Feel the fiery embers becoming ashes below your feet; It's time to spread your wings and fly my beautiful songbird, as you soar past this chapter in your life that caused you grief;"

El Roi (The God who sees me)

The Holy Spirit went on to say, "Now that you have been born again, I hope you look to me, your true best friend! For now you know, I hope you see, I never left you, it was you who had forgotten me;

"So If you ever find yourself again all alone in the dark, simply place your hand over your beating heart; Breathe in and out and know that I am real; Keep your faith and free will strong, something the enemy can never steal; Know that our bond can never be torn apart, feel my flame inside of your soul help ignite your spark!"

The Holy Spirit began to finish his profound message by saying, "I am now speaking directly to my precious child I see in front of me, and yes, that is you! For deep in your soul you always knew, when I said 'Tetelestai!' on the cross, my divine resurrection would liberate you! For I Am the Great I Am, the Alpha and Omega, with you always until the end of time; My dear child don't you see?

" I've held the keys to your eternal life from the very start;

For I am the living God, feel my love beating,

in the melody of your heart!"

Acknowledgments

I could not have completed this poem without my true best friend, Jesus Christ by my side. The Holy Spirit's love is truly transcending! I'm a walking miracle and want to spend my life glorifying my Heavenly Father. God wants our heart and for us to live a fulfilling life with him.

All of my love goes out to my friends and family who I've shared my testimony with and have supported me on this journey. You have heard my revisions of this poem countless times over the years and loved me unconditionally through the tears and healing. Thanks for believing in me and giving me the courage to share my heart and vulnerability with the world. I hope to bring a lantern into a dark place that can lead more people to God's light and give them a voice too. Thanks for making me feel seen, heard and valued. I love you all truly with all of my heart!

A special thank you to my dear friend, Jackie Schutza. Her photography evokes the emotion and dark beauty I wanted readers to feel in this hero's journey. All my love to her for seeing my vision, loving me unconditionally and meeting me where I was. You have my heart forever my soul sister!

My gratitude to Gauntlets of Love for allowing me to use your creative expression of art and writing on my dedication page. Your lighthouse quote embodies what we need more of in this world, compassion for ourselves and others. Thanks for shining your beacon!

A special thank you to the American Foundation for Suicide Prevention for allowing me to list them as a resource. They do amazing work as a non-proft for raising suicide awareness, providing free resources for people and fighting to end the stigma. If this is for you or a loved one, there is hope! I see your lamplight waiting to shine bright again, beautiful soul! There is strength in asking for help, so take that first step. You are not alone in your walk. Jesus is with you and he loves you very much!

"For I am persuaded that neither death, nor life, nor angels, nor principalities, nor powers, nor things present, nor things to come, nor height nor depth, nor any other creature, shall be able to separate us from the love of God which is in Christ Jesus our Lord."

Romans 8:38-39 (KJV)

Resources:

To learn more about suicide prevention and available resources for those who have lost loved ones to suicide, please visit the American Foundation for Suicide Prevention website at

afsp.org

talkawaythedark.afsp.org

If you or a loved one is having thoughts of suicide, please contact the 988 Suicide Crisis Lifeline by calling or texting

988 or text HOME to 741741

988Lifeline.org

About The Author

Jenny grew up in Austin, TX but has always found solace near the ocean and in nature. Growing up with a close relationship with Jesus Christ she would always feel his presence best in nature witnessing God's beautiful creation. She was blessed to get to live along the west coast for eight years. She loves writing prayers to God in the sand as she watches the waves carry them away feeling grounded near the sea.

She currently resides back in her hometown where she is now working in mental and behavioral health. She is also an active member of her church and serves on the prayer team and is continuing to grow in her faith journey. In her free time she enjoys spending quality time with her family and friends who she calls her soul family. She also enjoys hobbies such as hiking, painting, singing, playing piano, figure skating, and dance. She hopes to grow her own family one day but for now enjoys snuggle and play time with her beloved kitty Gabriella which means "God is my strength."

She has always enjoyed writing and journaling since she was little and felt poetry is an expressive outlet to speak from the soul in an artistic way. One of her long term goals includes continuing her self publishing journey to minister to people. She also has plans to travel and become a keynote speaker to advocate for suicide awareness and compassion fatigue prevention; Additional plans include using animal therapy to bring joy and be a light to people in their healing journey.

Made in the USA
Coppell, TX
11 October 2025